STATE OF THE ART PROGRAM

Portfolios

Robyn Montana Turner

BARRETT KENDALL PUBLISHING, Ltd.

AUSTIN, TEXAS

CREDITS

EDITORIAL

Project Director: *Linda Dunlap*

Senior Development Editor: *Linda Dunlap*

Editors: *Melissa Blackwell Burke, Claire Miller Colombo, Kathleen Fitzgibbon, Jody Frank, Mary Ann Frishman, Patty Moynahan, Tara Turner, Anne Walker*

Copy Editors: *Kathleen Unger, Sandra Wolfgang*

Editorial Support: *Mary Corbett, Elaine Clift Gore, Judy McBurney*

Administrative Manager: *Mark Blangger*

DESIGN, PRODUCTION, AND PHOTO RESEARCH

Project Director: *Pun Nio*

Designers: *Leslie Kell Designs, Jane Thurmond Designs, Pun Nio*

Design and Electronic Files: *Dodson Publication Services, Leslie Kell Designs, Jane Thurmond Designs, Linda Kensicki*

Photo Research: *Mark Blangger, Laurie O'Meara*

Photo Art Director: *Pun Nio*

Cover Design: *Leslie Kell Designs; Art Director, Pun Nio; Student Art: Sun, Clouds, and Flowers-Mai, Liestman Elementary; Cowboy-Danny, Boone Elementary; Fish-Alan, Conley Elementary; Puppet-Daisy, Campbell Elementary; Background-Brushworks Photo Disc*

Printed in the United States of America

ISBN 1-889105-10-4   2 3 4 5 6 7   VH 02 01 00 99 98

STATE OF THE ART PROGRAM

Portfolios

CONSULTANTS

Cindy G. Broderick, Ph.D.
Art Faculty
  Alamo Heights Junior School
  Alamo Heights Independent
    School District
  San Antonio, Texas

Sara Chapman, M.A.
Visual Arts Coordinator
  Alief Independent School District
  Houston, Texas

Brenda J. Chappell, Ph.D.
Art Consultant
  University of Tennessee
  Nashville, Tennessee

James Clarke, M.A.
*Program Director for Visual Arts and
Elementary Creative Drama*
  Aldine Independent School District
  Houston, Texas

Georgia Collins, Ph.D.
Professor, Department of Art
  University of Kentucky
  Lexington, Kentucky

Gloria Contreras, Ph.D.
*Professor, Department of Teacher
Education and Administration*
  University of North Texas
  Denton, Texas

Sandra M. Epps, Ph.D.
Director, Multicultural Programs
  Community School District Five
  New York, New York

Diane C. Gregory, Ph.D.
*Associate Professor of Art Education,
Department of Art and Design*
  Southwest Texas State University
  San Marcos, Texas

Susan M. Mayer, M.A.
*Coordinator of Museum Education,
Senior Lecturer of Art*
  The University of Texas at Austin
  Austin, Texas

Aaronetta Hamilton Pierce
Art Consultant
  African American Art and Artists
  San Antonio, Texas

Renee Sandell, Ph.D.
Professor, Department of Art Education
  Maryland Institute, College of Art
  Baltimore, Maryland

CONTRIBUTING WRITERS

Pamela Geiger Stephens, Ph.D.
Art Education Consultant
Colleyville, Texas

Sharon Warwick, M. Ed., M.S.A.
Art Specialist
Central Junior High School
Euless, Texas
Tarrant County Junior College
Hurst, Texas

Kay K. Wilson, M.A.
Art Consultant
North Texas Institute for Educators
on the Visual Arts
University of North Texas
Denton, Texas

REVIEWERS

Gini Robertson-Baker
Classroom Teacher
Bivins Elementary School
Amarillo Independent School District
Amarillo, Texas

Rosalinda Champion
Art Specialist
Edinburg Senior High School
Edinburg Consolidated School District
Edinburg, Texas

Margaret Jones
Classroom Teacher
Village Elementary School
Pittsburg Unified School District
Pittsburg, California

Nancy Mayeda
Principal, Creative Fine Arts
Magnet School
San Francisco Unified School District
San Francisco, California

Dana Reyna
Art Specialist
Odom Elementary School
Austin Independent School District
Austin, Texas

Ingrid Sherwood
Classroom Teacher
Reece Academy
Aldine Independent School District
Houston, Texas

Marilyn Wylie
Art Specialist
Conley Elementary School
Aldine Independent School District
Houston, Texas

iv

Art and You

Looking Closely

Art in Many Places

Thinking About Art

Unit 5

Art Old and New

More Ways to Do Art

Joan Miró. *Woman with Three Hairs Surrounded by Birds in the Night*. Palma, September 2, 1972. Oil on canvas, 95 ⅞ by 66½ inches (243.5 x 168.9 cm.). The Museum of Modern Art, New York. Gift of the artist in honor of James Thrall Soby. Photograph ©1996 The Museum of Modern Art, New York.

Art and You

Art is everywhere.
It can be many things.
It is a red wagon in the snow.

It is a cloud in the sky.

It is the wiggle in a puppy's tail.

Look around your world.
What kinds of art do you see?

First Look

Who is in the picture?
What is going on?
How does the picture make you feel?

Art words line shape artwork color

Lines in Your World

Lines are everywhere!
A line starts with a dot. ●
Then it grows.

Stephanie, Conley Elementary,
A Curly Orange Blue Painting.
Tempera on paper, 12 in. by 18 in.

F
Vinay, Heflin Elementary, *Untitled*.
Tempera on paper, 11 in. by 17 in.

Look at the pictures.
Which lines are straight?
Which ones curve?

Seeing Like an Artist

I can find lines on my clothes.
What types of lines do I see?

Lines in Your World 3

Pablo Picasso.
First Steps, 1943.
Oil on canvas,
51¼ by 38¼
inches. Yale
University Art
Gallery. Gift of
Stephen C. Clark,
B.A., 1903.

You Are Special

You are a special person.
What makes you feel special?
Who makes you feel special?

Vincent van Gogh. *First Steps, after Millet*, 1890. Oil on canvas, 28½ by 35⅞ inches. The Metropolitan Museum of Art, New York. Gift of George N. and Helen M. Richard, 1964. © The Metropolitan Museum of Art, New York.

Artists show feelings with lines.
How do the children feel?
What are these artists saying?
What types of lines do you see?

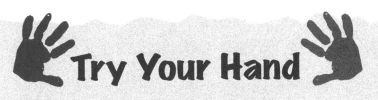

Try Your Hand

When do you feel special?
1. Draw you feeling special.
2. Use many types of lines.
3. Show your drawing to a friend.

Lines in Your World 5

Shapes in Your World

A Some lines make **shapes.**
Shapes are all around you.
Which shapes can you name?

B

C

D

Look around your room.
Which shapes do you see?
Artists use shapes.
You can, too.
Point to shapes in E.

Ruth, Amelia Earhart
Learning Center, *Shape
Collage.* Crayon, drawing
paper on paper, 8¾ in. by
12 in.

Planning Like an Artist

1. I can draw some shapes.
2. Then I'll cut them out.
3. I'll make some of them touch.
4. I'll move them around in different ways.

Which plan do I like best?

 John Biggers. *Family of Five*, 1985. Conte crayon, 24 by 18 inches. Courtesy of the artist.

Your Family Is Special

Artists draw and paint shapes.
Some drawings and paintings show families.
Drawings and paintings are called **artworks.**

Marisol Escobar. *The Family*, 1962. Painted wood and other materials in three sections, overall, 82⅝ by 65½ by 15½ inches. The Museum of Modern Art, New York. Advisory Committee Fund. Photograph ©1996 The Museum of Modern Art, New York.

Artists make many types of artworks.
Point to the shapes in **A** and **B**.
How are these families special?

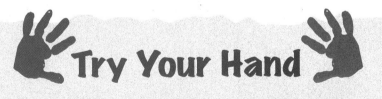

Try Your Hand

Use shapes to show your family.
1. Cut some shapes.
2. Move them around.
3. Glue your best design.
4. Show your artwork to a friend.

Colors in Your World

Artists mix **colors.**
You can, too!
What colors make orange?
What colors make **violet?**
What colors make green?

Alan, Conley Elementary, *The Sun with Eyebrows*. Tempera on black paper, 18 in. by 24 in.

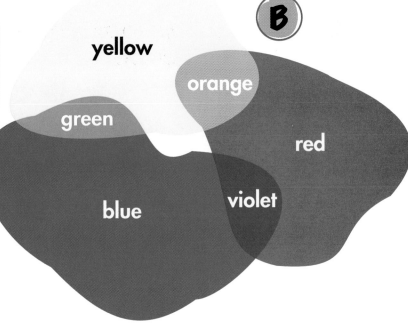

yellow
orange
green
red
blue
violet

B

C

How to
Use Your Paintbrush

1. Wash it.

2. Wipe it.

3. Blot it.

4. Go to another color.

 E

Amanda, Anderson Academy, *Long Tall Texan.* Tempera, crayon on paper, 11¾ in. by 17⅞ in.

Artists paint colors in their world.
You can paint colors, too.

Thinking Like an Artist

My friends are wearing colors.
How many colors can I name?
What colors am I wearing?

Maria
Sam
Latesha
Travis

Paul Klee. *Runner at the Goal*, 1921. Watercolor and gouache, 11⅞ by 9 inches. Solomon R. Guggenheim Museum, New York. Photograph by David Heald, ©The Solomon R. Guggenheim Foundation, New York.

Everyone Is Special

Everyone in the world is special.
Artists show this with lines, shapes, and colors.
They use colors in different ways.
Look at **A**.
Point to dark colors.
Point to light ones.
Is the runner happy? Why?

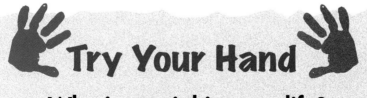

Rufino Tamayo. *Danza de la Alegria (Dance of Joy)*, 1950. Oil on canvas, 41⅞ by 28 inches. Photograph ©1996 Sotheby's, Inc., New York. Reproduction authorized by the Olga and Rufino Tamayo Foundation, A.C.

Look at **B**.
What colors did the artist use?
How does the dancer feel?
Why?

Try Your Hand

Who is special in your life?
Paint a picture with colors.

PORTFOLIO PROJECT

My Shape

How will you show your own shape?

1. Lie down on a piece of paper. Ask a friend to draw around you.

2. Color your shape.

3. Cut it out.

Who can guess which shape is yours?
How do you like your artwork?
Would you keep it the same?
Would you change it?

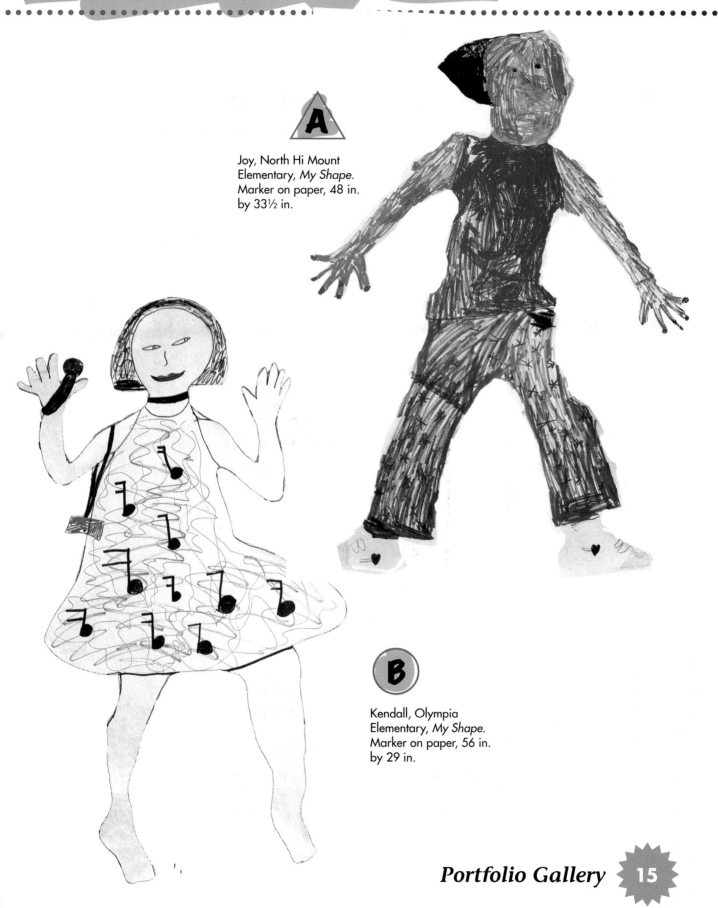

A

Joy, North Hi Mount Elementary, *My Shape*. Marker on paper, 48 in. by 33½ in.

B

Kendall, Olympia Elementary, *My Shape*. Marker on paper, 56 in. by 29 in.

TALK ABOUT ART

A Balthus, Baltusz Klossowski de Rola. *Joan Miró and His Daughter Dolores*, 1937-38. Oil on canvas, 51¼ by 35 inches (130.2 by 88.9 cm.). The Museum of Modern Art, New York. Abby Aldrich Rockefeller Fund. Photograph ©1996 The Museum of Modern Art, New York.

B

Joan Miró. Detail of *Woman with Three Hairs Surrounded by Birds in the Night*. Palma, September 2, 1972. Oil on canvas, 95⅞ by 66½ inches (243.5 x 168.9 cm.). The Museum of Modern Art, New York. Gift of the artist in honor of James Thrall Soby. Photograph ©1996 The Museum of Modern Art, New York.

Picture **A** shows a father with his daughter.
The father painted **B**.

Name the colors in **B**.
Point to different shapes.
Do some lines make you laugh? Why?

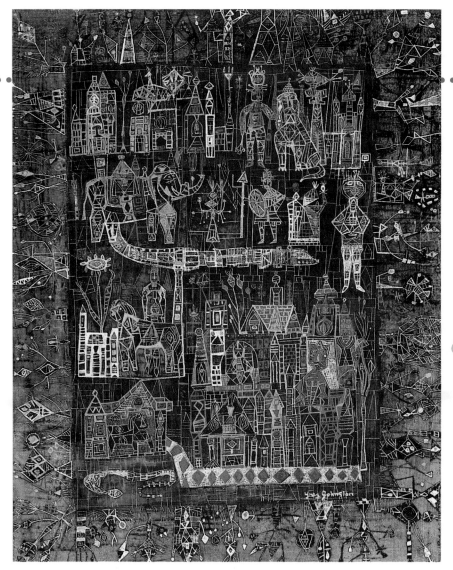

Ynez Johnston. *Dark Jungle*, 1950. Casein on cardboard, 23⅞ by 18½ inches. (60.6 by 47 cm.). The Museum of Modern Art, New York. Katharine Cornell Fund. Photograph ©1996 The Museum of Modern Art, New York.

What is happening in **C**?
Are the animals large or small?
Point to straight and curved lines.
Which shapes do you see?

Which artworks look close up?
Which one looks far away?
What does each picture mean to you?
How does each picture make you feel?
Have your feelings about **B** and **C** changed
since you first saw them? Explain.

Unit 1 17

WRITE ABOUT ART

Miró looked closely at things.

He looked at  .

He looked at  .

He looked at  .

He watched the  and the  .

He began to  things around him.

He used  in new ways.

He used  to show things.

He being an artist.

Look closely at things around you.
Choose one of them to draw.
Use lines, shapes, and colors.

Write some words about your drawing.

What Have You Learned?

Where have you seen these pictures?

1. Point to straight lines.
2. Point to curved lines.
3. What other lines can you find?

4. Can you find squares?
5. What other shapes can you find?
6. Name the colors in **C**.

7. Which art activity did you enjoy? Why?
8. Turn back to the artwork you like best.
9. Tell why you like it.
10. What else have you learned about art and you?

Art and You

Jean-Baptiste-Siméon Chardin. *Soap Bubbles*, probably 1733/1734. Oil on canvas, 36⅝ by 29⅜ inches.
©1996 Board of Trustees, National Gallery of Art, Washington, D.C. Gift of Mrs. John W. Simpson.

Looking Closely

Artists look closely at things around them.
They look at lines in a sea shell.

They look at shapes of
windows and doors.

They look at colors on a turtle's back.

You are an artist.
What will you look for?

 **First Look**

What is the man doing?
Who is watching?
Will the child blow a bubble, too?

Art words **texture pattern detail**
warm colors cool colors

Discovering Textures

A

B

These pictures show **texture.**
Texture can feel rough or smooth.
Touching things can help you learn.
Try to guess how these things feel.

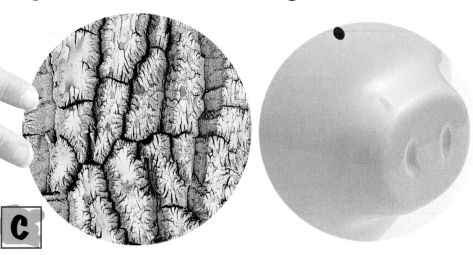

C

1. Fold and mark.

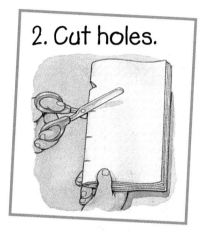

2. Cut holes.

3. Weave yarn in and out.

4. Weave it again.

5. Tie the yarn.

D Sarah, Olympia Elementary, *My Sketchbook*. Oil pastels on const. paper, yarn, 12 in. by 9 in.

Where can you look for textures?
Are they rough or smooth?

Seeing Like an Artist

**How can I show rough texture?
I could use lines and shapes.
I could draw them in my sketchbook.**

Discovering Textures **23**

Albrecht Dürer. *Rhinoceros*, 1515. Woodcut, 9¼ by 11¾ inches. Prints Collection Miriam and Ira D. Wallach Division of Art, Prints and Photography, New York Public Library, Astor, Lenox and Tilden Foundation.

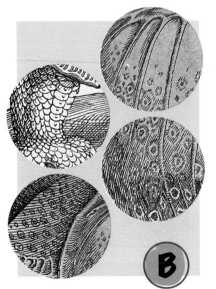

Textures in Animals

Animals have textures.
They can be hard or soft.
They can be rough or smooth.
Point to textures on **A**, **C**, and **D**.

How did the artist show textures?
Point to lines and shapes.

 Rosa Bonheur. *The King of the Desert*, 19th century. Oil on canvas, 39⅜ by 37⅝ inches. Courtesy of Sotheby's, Inc., New York.

 Artist unknown. Detail of *Calligraphy: Young Lion*, 19th century, U.S. Pen and brown ink, 18 by 24 inches. M. and M. Karolik Collection. Courtesy, Museum of Fine Arts, Boston. 60.1118

An artist painted **C**.
Another artist drew **D**.
What textures did they show?
Are the textures hard or soft?
Are they rough or smooth?

Try Your Hand

Draw or paint a big animal.
It can be real or imaginary.
Show some textures on it.
What is your animal's name?

Finding Patterns

A

B Jacob, Woodridge Elementary, *Untitled.*
Tempera on paper, 21¼ in. by 24¼ in.

C

Repeated lines make **patterns.**

Repeated shapes make patterns, too.

Point to patterns in these pictures.
Can you find patterns in your room?

Many Ways to Make Patterns

Draw

Print

Paint

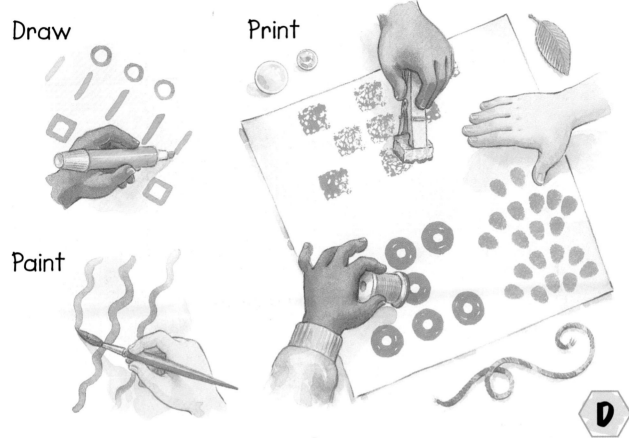

It is easy to make patterns.
You can draw or paint them.
You can even print them.
What patterns will you make?

Planning Like an Artist

I can plan to make some patterns.
I could try many ways.
I can draw, paint, or print.

 Carmen Lomas Garza. *Abuelitos Piscando Nopalitos (Grandparents Harvesting Cactus)*, 1980. Gouache painting, 11 by 14 inches. ©1980 Carmen Lomas Garza. Collection of Richard L. Bains and Amalia Mesa-Bains, San Francisco, Calif.

Patterns in Family Pictures

This artist shows her mother and grandfather.
She shows her grandmother and brother.
They are all working together.
What are they picking?
What patterns can you find?
Which lines and shapes make these patterns?

B

Carmen Lomas Garza.
Abuelitos Piscando Nopalitos (Detail)

C

Carmen Lomas Garza.
Abuelitos Piscando Nopalitos (Detail)

D

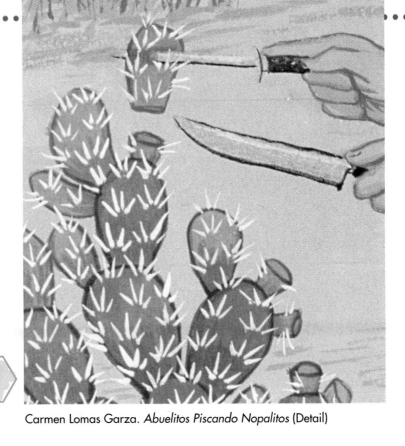

Carmen Lomas Garza. *Abuelitos Piscando Nopalitos* (Detail)

Picture **B** shows a close-up view.
So do **C** and **D**.
Close-up views can help you see **details.**
Details are small parts.
Point to some details in **B**, **C**, and **D**.

Try Your Hand

Show your family working together.
Draw, paint, or print some patterns.
Add some details.

Seeing Warm and Cool Colors

A

B

Warm colors

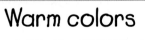

C

D Jimmy, Woodridge Elementary, *Untitled.* Tempera on paper, 20½ in. by 11¾ in.

Colors have families, too.
One color family has **warm colors**.
Another color family has **cool colors**.
Artists use warm and cool colors.

Rollie, Woodridge Elementary, *Colorful Design*. Tempera on heavy paper, 14 in. by 11 in.

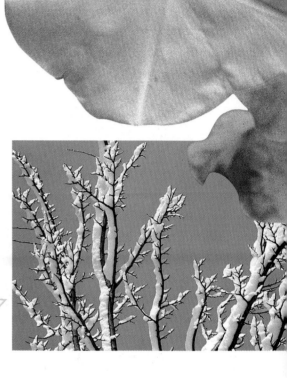

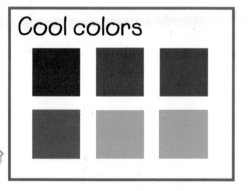

Cool colors

Which pictures show warm colors?
Which pictures show cool colors?
Which pictures show both?

Thinking Like an Artist

I might draw a warm place.
Which color family would I choose?
Why do artists choose their colors?

Seeing Warm and Cool Colors   31

 Janet Fish. *Jonathan and Lorraine*, 1988. Oil on canvas, 64 by 72¾ inches. Abudefduf, Inc., New York.

Colors Can Show Feelings

Some artists paint about feelings.
They choose color families to help them.
Find warm colors in **A**.
How do they make you feel?

Find cool colors in **B**.
How do they make you feel?

Try Your Hand

Think of a strong feeling you have had.
Why did you feel that way?
Paint a picture of you then.
Choose colors to show how you felt.

Seeing Warm and Cool Colors

PORTFOLIO PROJECT

Rubbing of a Wild Animal
How many textures can you find?

1. Draw and cut large shapes.

   1 square

   3 circles

   6 triangles

   1 rectangle

2. Rub textures. Use warm colors. Press down hard.

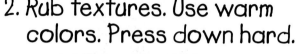

3. Move your shapes around. Paste them down to make an animal.

4. Add details.

How many textures did you rub?
Which colors did you use?
What will you name your wild animal?

PORTFOLIO GALLERY

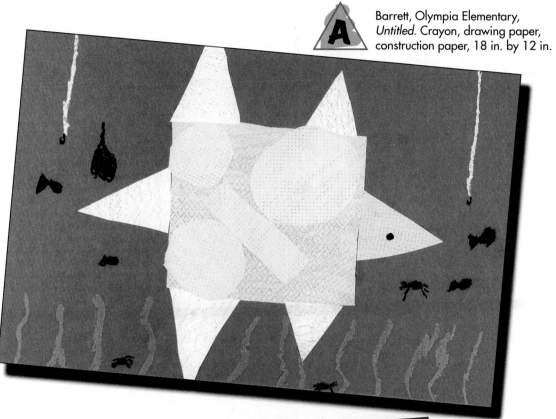

A Barrett, Olympia Elementary, *Untitled*. Crayon, drawing paper, construction paper, 18 in. by 12 in.

B LaTonya, Olympia Elementary, *Untitled*. Crayon, drawing paper, construction paper, 18 in. by 12 in.

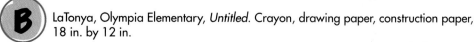

TALK ABOUT ART

 Jean-Baptiste-Siméon Chardin. *Self-portrait with pincenez,* 1771. Oil on canvas, 17¾ by 14¾ inches. The Louvre, Paris, France. Photograph © Erich Lessing, Art Resource, New York.

 Jean-Baptiste-Siméon Chardin, Detail of *Soap Bubbles,* probably 1733/1734. Oil on canvas, 36⅝ by 29⅜ inches. © 1996 Board of Trustees, National Gallery of Art, Washington, D.C. Gift of Mrs. John W. Simpson.

Picture **A** shows the artist.
He painted both **A** and **B**.
What might the artist be thinking in **A**?

What is the small boy doing in **B**?
Point to several details in **B**.

 Chinese, Northern Song dynasty. Detail of *Court Ladies Preparing Newly Woven Silk* (detail: *Women Combing Silk*), early 12th century. Attributed to the Emperor Hui-zong. Handscroll: ink, colors, and gold on silk, 14½ by 17⅝ inches. Chinese and Japanese Special Fund. Courtesy of Museum of Fine Arts, Boston.

What is the small girl doing in **C**?
What does she see?
What texture do you see?
Point to patterns.
Where do you see warm colors?

What do both artists show about children?
What does each picture mean to you?
Have your feelings about **B** and **C** changed since
you first saw them? Explain.

WRITE ABOUT ART

Chardin painted   of life in

his town.

He showed  working.

He painted pictures of  playing.

This artist liked to paint pictures of .

He also painted pictures of .

Sometimes he painted with his .

Look at **B** on page 36.

What will happen to the  ?

Have you watched someone blow bubbles?
Did you ever blow a bubble?
What happened to the bubble?

Write some words about bubbles.
Draw a bubble around your words.

What Have You Learned?

Where have you seen these pictures?

1. Find a rough texture.
2. Name other textures you see.
3. Point to a pattern made with lines.
4. Point to a pattern made with shapes.

5. Which pictures show close-up views?
6. Where do you see warm colors?
7. Name the colors in **C**.

8. Which activity was your favorite?
9. Which of your artworks do you like best?
10. Tell why you like it.
11. Tell about your friend's best artwork.

12. What else did you learn about looking closely?

Albrecht Dürer. Detail of *Rhinoceros*, 1515. Woodcut, 9¼ by 11¾ inches. Prints Collection Miriam and Ira D. Wallach Division of Art, Prints and Photography, New York Public Library, Astor, Lenox and Tilden Foundation.

Carmen Lomas Garza. Detail of *Abuelitos Piscando Nopalitos (Grandparents Harvesting Cactus)*, 1980. Gouache painting, 11 by 14 inches. ©1980 Carmen Lomas Garza. Collection of Richard L. Bains and Amalia Mesa-Bains, San Francisco, Calif.

Janet Fish. Detail of *Jonathan and Lorraine*, 1988. Oil on canvas, 64 by 72¾ inches. Abudefduf, Inc., New York.

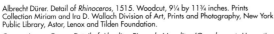

Looking Closely **39**

Felipe Benito Archuleta. *Baboon*, 1978. Carved and painted cottonwood and pine with glue and sawdust, 16½ by 42½ by 13 inches. National Museum of American Art, Hemphill Collection, Smithsonian Institution, Washington, D.C. Gift of Herbert Waide Hemphill, Jr., and museum purchase made possible by Ralph Cross Johnson. ©1978, Felipe Archuleta. Art Resource, New York.

Art in Many Places

You've seen that art is in many places.
It is indoors and outdoors.
It is large and small.
It is old and new.

Some artworks have
only one side to see.

Others have more than one side
to see.

First Look

What animal is in the picture?
What does it have in its mouth?
Suppose this artwork were in your room.
Could you go around it?

Art words **form space sculpture sculptor
movement puppet original**

Forms Take Up Space

All **forms** take up **space.**
You are a form.
How much space do you take up?

Look at **A**.
What is in front of the girl?
What is behind her?
Point to what is above and below her.
Which animals are beside her?

B **Types of Forms**

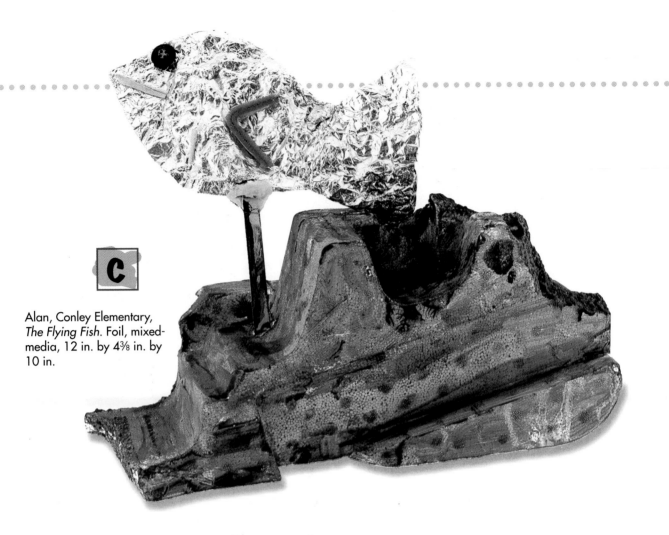

Alan, Conley Elementary,
The Flying Fish. Foil, mixed-
media, 12 in. by 4⅜ in. by
10 in.

The girl in **A** is a form.
The artwork in **C** is a form, too.
You can go around both of them.

Seeing Like an Artist

I can find forms in my classroom.
Which things can I go around?

Forms Take Up Space **43**

Artist unknown (Nigerian). *Pair of Ivory Leopards*, 19th century. Ivory and copper, 34⁹⁄₁₆ by 18½ inches (left), 33-7/16 by 18-1/2 inches (right). By kind permission of The Lord Chamberlain's Office, image supplied by The Trustees of the British Museum.

Artists and Forms

Some artists make **sculptures**.
These artists are called **sculptors**.

Sculptures are forms.
Look at **A**, **B**, **C**, and **D**.
They are sculptures.
Could you go around them?
Name the animals in **A**.
Point to patterns and textures on them.

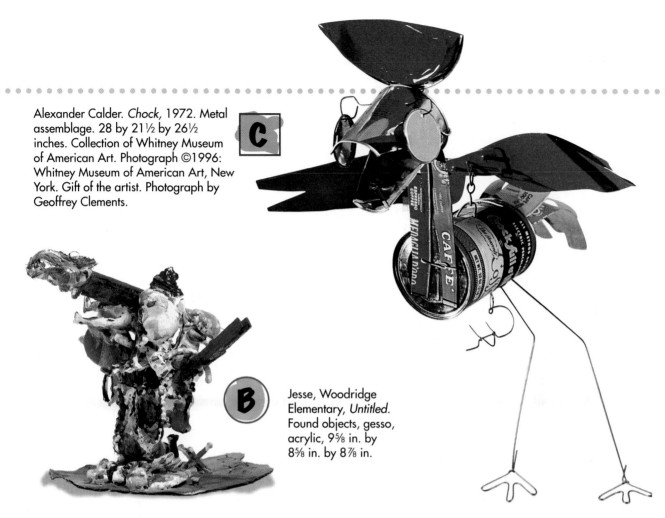

Alexander Calder. *Chock,* 1972. Metal assemblage. 28 by 21½ by 26½ inches. Collection of Whitney Museum of American Art. Photograph ©1996: Whitney Museum of American Art, New York. Gift of the artist. Photograph by Geoffrey Clements.

C

B Jesse, Woodridge Elementary, *Untitled.* Found objects, gesso, acrylic, 9⅝ in. by 8⅝ in. by 8⅞ in.

Some sculptors save things they find.
They put them together as sculptures.
Their imaginations help them.
Point to **C**.
What does it look like?

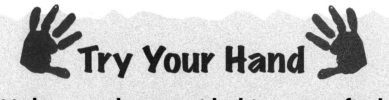

Try Your Hand

Make a sculpture with things you find.
Your teacher will show you how.
Will your sculpture show a real animal?
Will your animal be imaginary?

Forms Take Up Space **45**

Action All Around

Action happens all around you.
Almost everything moves.
Some things move fast.
Others move slowly.
They all have **movement.**
How can you show movement?

A

B

C

D

E

F

Danny, Boone Elementary,
Calf Ropin'. Watered tempera,
marker, 11 in. by 17 in.

These pictures show movement.
Which lines help you see action?
Can you feel the movement? Tell why.

Planning Like an Artist

I can see movement all around me.
I can draw lines that show movement.
I'll draw in my sketchbook.
What colors shall I choose?

 Henry Moore. *Rocking Chair No. 2*, 1950. Bronze, 11⅛ by 12⅜ by 3¼ inches. Hirshhorn Museum and Sculpture Garden, Smithsonian Institution, Washington, D.C. Gift of Joseph H. Hirshhorn, 1966. Photograph by Lee Stalsworth.

Artists Can Show Movement

Some sculptors like to show movement.
Which sculpture shows slow movement?
Which sculpture shows fast movement?
Point to lines that show movement.

Abastenia St. Leger Eberle. *Roller Skating*,
c.1906. Bronze, 12¹³⁄₁₆ by 11¼ by 6½ inches.
Photograph ©1996 Whitney Museum of American
Art, New York. Gift of Gertrude Vanderbilt Whitney.
Photograph by Geoffrey Clements.

Can you show how the chair moves in **A**?
Can you feel the wind blow in **C**?

Try Your Hand

**Make a sculpture of yourself.
What will you be doing?
How will you show movement?**

Action All Around   49

Many Kinds of Puppets

Bamana People (Mali). *Puppets*, c.1960. Painted wood with metal, height 43 inches (tallest). From the Girard Foundation Collection in the Museum of International Folk Art, a unit of the Museum of New Mexico, Santa Fe, N.Mex. Photograph by Michel Monteaux.

A

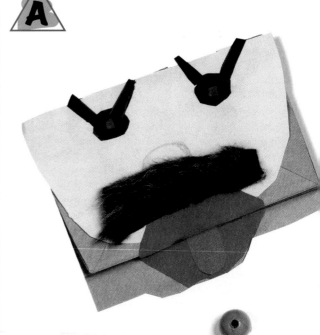

B

Rosbelia, Campbell Elementary, *Buttons and Whiskers*. Paper sack, construction paper, buttons, imitation fur, 6½ in. by 12½ in.

Some artists like to make **puppets.**
Puppets are forms, too.
Do puppets take up space?
Can you go around a puppet?

How to
Make a Sack Puppet

c

1. Cut out shapes for eyes, nose, mouth.

2. Paste them onto the bottom of the sack.

3. Add some hair.

4. Add the rest.

Artists create many types of puppets.
Each puppet is different from all others.
Each puppet is an **original** artwork.
Artists like to create original artworks.

Thinking Like an Artist

How can I create an original puppet?
I could think of my own ideas.
Mine will be different from others.

You Can Make Puppets Move

Puppets can show movement.
You can make them jump.
You can make them dance.

Artist unknown (Indonesia). *Shadow Puppet*, c. 1950. Cut painted leather, height 31½ inches. From the Girard Foundation Collection in the Museum of International Folk Art, a unit of the Museum of New Mexico, Santa Fe, N.Mex. Photograph by Michel Monteaux.

Artist unknown (India). *Marionettes: Sword Fighter and Dancer*, c. 1900. Painted wood and cloth, height 22 inches. From the Girard Foundation Collection in the Museum of International Folk Art, a unit of the Museum of New Mexico, Santa Fe, N.Mex. Photograph by Michel Monteaux.

D

Daisy, Campbell Elementary, *Red Lips*. Paper sack, construction paper, string, 6½ in by 12½ in.

C

You can have a puppet show.
What story will you tell?
What will your puppets say?
Who will help you?

Try Your Hand

Make a sack puppet.
Plan a puppet show.
Ask your friends to help you.
Who will come to your show?

E

Jessica, Campbell Elementary, *Purple Ears*. Paper sack, construction paper, yarn, crayon, 6½ in. by 12½ in.

PORTFOLIO PROJECT

Making Zoo Animals with Clay

Think of an animal you like.
Is it real or imaginary?

1. Make a head and body.	2. Add the face.	3. Make the other parts.
	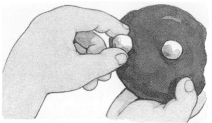	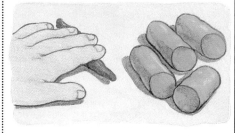
4. Gently press them together.	5. Make some fur or feathers.	6. Put it all together.

Does your animal stand up?
Does it have space around it?
Can you plan with your friends?
Will you make a zoo together?

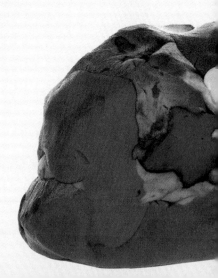

PORTFOLIO GALLERY

Kiokyo, Olympia Elementary,
Turtle. Modeling clay, 4 in. by
5 in. by 2 in.

Tyler, Olympia Elementary,
Lion. Modeling clay, 6 in.
by 2¾ in. by 3½ in.

TALK ABOUT ART

Davis Mather. *Felipe B. Archuleta and Gorilla*, 1976. Photograph ©Davis Mather, Santa Fe, N.Mex.

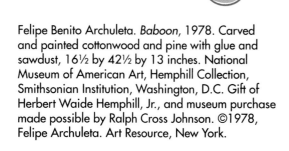

B

Felipe Benito Archuleta. *Baboon*, 1978. Carved and painted cottonwood and pine with glue and sawdust, 16½ by 42½ by 13 inches. National Museum of American Art, Hemphill Collection, Smithsonian Institution, Washington, D.C. Gift of Herbert Waide Hemphill, Jr., and museum purchase made possible by Ralph Cross Johnson. ©1978, Felipe Archuleta. Art Resource, New York.

The artist in **A** was a sculptor.
He made **B**.
Does **B** look rough or smooth?

C

Pablo Picasso. *Baboon and Young*, Vallauris, 1951. Bronze (cast 1955), after found objects, 21 by 13¼ by 20¾ inches (53.3 by 33.3 by 52.7 cm.). The Museum of Modern Art, New York. Mrs. Simon Guggenheim Fund. Photograph ©1996 The Museum of Modern Art, New York.

Name the large animal in **C**.
How did the sculptor make its head?
Point to the small animal in **C**.
Could you tell that **C** is an artwork from all sides?

Does **B** or **C** show movement?
Which baboon is walking on four legs?

How are the tails different in **B** and **C**?
What were the sculptors saying about animals?
Have your feelings about **B** and **C** changed since you first saw them? Explain.

WRITE ABOUT ART

Archuleta lived in New Mexico.

He worked hard with his  .

He picked fruit in the hot .

He helped build   .

But he wanted to become a  .

He began to make   from wood.

He would  the sculptures.

Sometimes he added , cloth, or straw.

He won many  for his art.

Think about making a wooden cat.
What could you use for whiskers?
What could you use for the tail?
What could you use for the nose?

Write some sentences.
Tell how you would make your cat.

What Have You Learned?

Where have you seen these pictures?

1. Which pictures show close-up views?

2. Which artworks have a hard texture?

3. Point to the artwork with colorful patterns.

4. Point to a sculpture that shows movement.

5. Point to a funny sculpture.

6. Which artworks are forms?

7. How many of these artworks are original?

8. Which art activity did you like?

9. Why did you like it?

10. Turn back to the artwork you like best.

11. Tell why you like it.

12. What else have you learned about art in many places?

Alexander Calder. Detail of *Chock,* 1972. Metal assemblage. 28 by 21½ by 26½ inches. Collection of Whitney Museum of American Art. Photograph ©1996: Whitney Museum of American Art, New York. Gift of the artist. Photograph by Geoffrey Clements.

Abastenia St. Leger Eberle. Detail of *Roller Skating,* c.1906. Bronze, 12¹³⁄₁₆ by 11¼ by 6½ inches. Photograph ©1996 Whitney Museum of American Art, New York. Gift of Gertrude Vanderbilt Whitney. Photograph by Geoffrey Clements.

Artist unknown (Indonesia). Detail of *Shadow Puppet,* c. 1950. Cut painted leather, height 31½ inches. From the Girard Foundation Collection in the Museum of International Folk Art, a unit of the Museum of New Mexico, Santa Fe, N.Mex. Photograph by Michel Monteaux.

Art in Many Places

Mary Cassatt. Detail of *Little Girl in a Blue Armchair*, 1878. Oil on canvas, 35¼ by 51⅛ inches. ©1996 Board of Trustees, National Gallery of Art, Washington, D.C. Collection of Mr. and Mrs. Paul Mellon.

Thinking About Art

People think in many ways.
They think by looking.
They think by remembering.
They think by imagining.

Artists look, remember, and imagine.
This helps them create artworks.

What helps you create artworks?

First Look

What is the girl thinking about?
What could she be looking at?
What might she be remembering?
Could she be imagining?

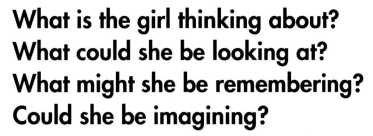

 **Art words**

senses   balance
symmetrical   prints   face
portrait   self-portrait
architect

Finding What's Important

 Franz Marc. *Yellow Cow*, 1911. Oil on canvas. Solomon R. Guggenheim Museum, New York. Photo by David Heald. ©The Solomon R. Guggenheim Foundation, New York. (FN49.1210)

Look at the pictures on these pages.
Point to things that catch your eye.
What do you see first in **A**?
Tell why.

B) Adrian, Anderson Academy, *Horse at Night*.
Tempera, crapas, ink on paper, 17 ¾ in. by 12 in.

Artists try to show what is important.
What do you see first in **B**?
What is the artist trying to say?

Seeing Like an Artist

What is important to me?
How can I show this in my artwork?
I could make it large.
I could use bright colors.

A

Paul Gauguin. *Still Life with Three Puppies,* 1888. Oil on wood, 36⅛ by 24⅝ inches (91.8 by 62.6 cm.). The Museum of Modern Art, New York. Mrs. Simon Guggenheim Fund. Photograph ©1996 The Museum of Modern Art, New York.

Everyone Needs Food

Puppies and people need food.
How did the artists show that food is important?

B

Ebony, Campbell Elementary, *Picnic at the Park.* Tempera, magazine photos on paper, 18 in by 12 in.

 Diego Rivera. *Orchard with Children Scene*, 1931. Fresco, 62¼ by 104¾ inches. Stern Hall, University of California at Berkeley. Photographed with permission of the Regents of University of California at Berkeley by Don Beatty ©1983.

Artists use **senses** to help them learn.
So do you.
Which picture shows tasting?
Which pictures show touching?
Which other senses help you learn?

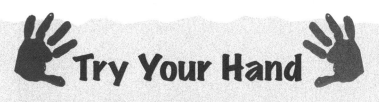

Try Your Hand

Imagine the perfect picnic.
1. Paint a place for a picnic.
2. Cut and paste pictures of food.
3. Add people.
What is important in your picture?

Discovering Balance

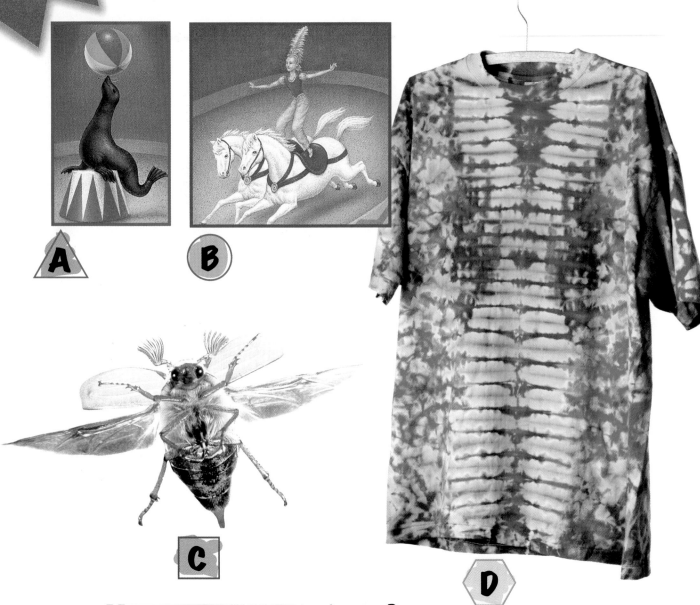

Have you seen a circus?
Seals balance balls on their noses.
Performers balance with their arms.
Look at **C** and **D**.
Are both sides of each one about the same?
Artists use **symmetrical balance** in their artworks.

E How to
Make A Print

1. Fold it.

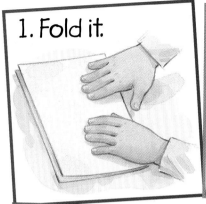

2. Paint it.

3. Close it.

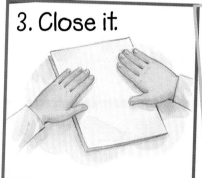

4. Name it. Hang it up.

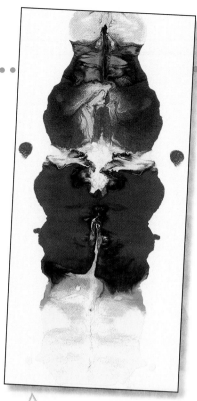

F Christopher, Forest Trail Elementary, *Bunny Brothers.* Tempera on paper 11⅞ in. by 9 in.

Artists make symmetrical **prints.**
You can, too.
Look at the print in F.
What type of balance does it show?

Planning Like an Artist

Where will I hang my print?
I can choose a place.
My teacher could help me.

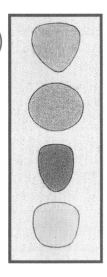

Everyone Needs Clothing

People wear many types of clothing.
It protects them from the weather.
Tell about the clothing in **A**.
How is it different from clothing in **C**?

All of these pictures are **portraits.**
They each show a picture of someone.
Picture **A** is a **self-portrait.**
The artist painted a picture of herself.
What is she holding?

 Unidentified artist. *Man wearing coat with tiger rank badge signifying that he is a fourth-degree military official,* probably K'ang-hsi period (1662-1723). Color and ink on paper,13 ⅛ by 14 ⅛ inches. The Metropolitan Museum of Art, New York. Anonymous gift, 1952. ©1980, The Metropolitan Museum of Art.

 Nadia, Conley Elementary, *Untitled.* Tempera, crayon on paper, 18 in. by 12 in.

Look at **faces** in all of these pictures.
You can see some face shapes in **B**.
The artists used different shapes.
What shape is your face?

Try Your Hand

Make a portrait.
1. Fold the paper.
2. Make a print for clothing.
3. Draw a face on the fold.
4. Draw arms and legs.
5. Add details.
What type of balance does your artwork show?

Exploring Shapes and Spaces

A

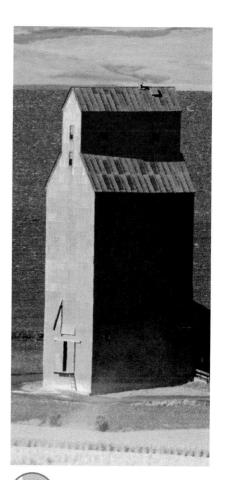
B

C

Pictures come in many shapes.
Point to a tall picture.
Now find a wide one.
Can you see a round one?
Artists plan the shapes of their pictures.

Artists fill their pictures.
They use space in many ways.
How did all of these artists fill their space?

Thinking Like an Artist

What shapes will I make my pictures?
I'll sketch some ideas.
How do I want to fill the shapes?
I can use space in many ways.

A

Gabriele Münter,
*The Russian House
(Das Russen-Haus),*
1931. Oil on
canvas, 16¾ by
22½ inches.
Städtische Galerie
im Lenbachhaus,
Munich, Germany.

Everyone Needs Shelter

Shelters are places to live and work.
They protect you from the outside world.
Look at the shelter in **A**.
Point to light colors.
Now find some dark ones.

The artist mixed paints to make these colors.
You can, too.

B

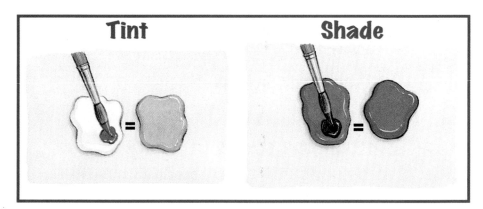

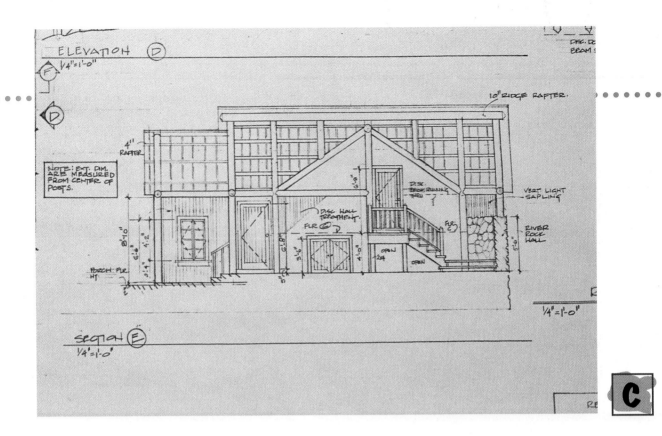

Architects plan how to build shelters.
These artists draw their plans.
The plans show shapes in shelters.
Picture **C** shows an architect's plan.
Name some shapes in **A** and **C**.

Try Your Hand

Paint a picture of a new school building.
1. Mix light and dark colors.
2. Paint a large shape for your building.
3. Paint small shapes for windows and doors.
What other shapes will you use?

PORTFOLIO PROJECT

Outdoor Spaces

Look around outdoors.
Where are light and dark colors?

1. Mix some light colors. 	2. Mix some dark colors. 
3. Paint the sky and the ground. Let your painting dry. 	4. Cut out an animal. Paste it on. 

Add some details.

Point to your light colors.
Point to your dark colors.
Why does your animal look important?
Would you change anything?

PORTFOLIO GALLERY

A

Jessie, Conley Elementary, *Beautiful Colors*. Tempera, wallpaper on paper, 18 in. by 12 in.

B

Ericka, Conley Elementary, *Snake in the Valley*. Tempera, wallpaper on paper, 18 in. by 12 in.

TALK ABOUT ART

 Mary Cassatt. *Self-Portrait*, c.1880. Watercolor on paper, 13 by 9⅝ inches (33 by 24.4 cm.). The National Portrait Gallery, Smithsonian Institution. Art Resource, New York.

Look at **A**.
It is a self-portrait.
The artist in **A** painted **A** and **B**.
What is her name?

 Mary Cassatt. *Little Girl in a Blue Armchair*, 1878. Oil on canvas, 35½ by 51⅛ inches. © 1996 Board of Trustees, National Gallery of Art, Washington, D.C. Collection of Mr. and Mrs. Paul Mellon.

What animal is with the girl in **B**?
What else do you see in the room?
Try to imagine what you might hear.

 Peter Hurd. *Eve of St. John*, 1960. Tempera on board, 28 by 48 inches (71 by 121.9 cm.). San Diego Museum of Art. Gift of Mr. and Mrs. Norton S. Walbridge. 1975:069

Look at **C**.
What is important in this picture?
How did the artist show this?
What might the girl be thinking?

Look at **B** and **C**.
Which portrait is indoors?
Which one is outdoors?
Which picture shows an open space?
Are the girls close up or far away?

What do you think each artist was trying to say?
Have your feelings about **B** and **C** changed since you first saw them? Explain.

WRITE ABOUT ART

Cassatt painted pictures of  .

She painted pictures of  at  .

She painted pictures of  at the  .

One picture shows a in a  .

The seems to be resting.

There is a in the picture.

The seems to be resting, too.

Maybe they have been  .

Draw a picture of a child and a dog.
They might be playing outside.
They might be resting together.
You might add something funny.

Write about your drawing.

What Have You Learned?

Where have you seen these pictures?

A B C

1. Point to a self-portrait.
2. Which picture is about tasting?
3. Point to a shelter.
4. What type of balance does **C** show?

5. Name the light colors you see.
6. Where do you see warm colors?

7. Find some squares.
8. Where is a triangle?
9. Point to curved lines.

10. Turn back to the artwork you like best.
11. Tell why you like it.

12. What else have you learned about thinking about art?

Paul Gauguin. *Still Life with Three Puppies*, 1888. Oil on wood, 36⅛ by 24⅝ inches (91.8 by 62.6 cm.). The Museum of Modern Art, New York. Mrs. Simon Guggenheim Fund. Photograph ©1996 The Museum of Modern Art, New York.

Frida Kahlo (Mexican, 1907-1954). *Self-Portrait Dedicated to Leon Trotsky*, 1937. Oil on masonite, 30 by 24 inches. The National Museum of Women in the Arts. Gift of the Honorable Clare Booth Luce.

Gabriele Münter, *The Russian House (Das Russen-Haus)*, 1931. Oil on canvas, 16¾ by 22½ inches. Städtische Galerie im Lenbachhaus, Munich, Germany.

Thinking About Art 79

Rosa Bonheur. Detail of *Rabbits Nibbling Carrots*, 1840. Oil on canvas, 21¼ by 25½ in. Bordeaux Musée des Beaux-Arts. Reproduction © Musée des Beaux-Arts de Bordeaux.

Art Old and New

Artworks from long ago tell about life then.
They help you learn about the past.

New artworks tell about life now.
What do new artworks help you learn?

Artists today look at old and new artworks.
They get new ideas.
They try different ways of making things.
What can you learn from old and new art?

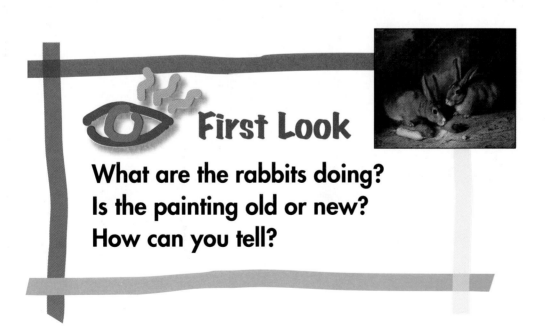

First Look

What are the rabbits doing?
Is the painting old or new?
How can you tell?

Art words   photograph   camera   motion
illustrate   museum   model

Photographs Then and Now

A

B

Look at **B** and **C**.
They are **photographs**.
The artists took them with a **camera**.

Picture **B** shows black, white, and gray.
Is the photograph old or new?
How can you tell?

C

Artists look through their cameras to plan.
They find what pleases their eye.

Pictures **B** and **C** show the same street.
How are they alike?
How are they different?
What was each artist trying to say?

Seeing Like an Artist

What might I see through a camera?
I can use my finger and thumb.
They can help me see.
I can cover my other eye.
Now I can plan a photograph.

D

Photographs Then and Now

A

B

Jessica, Woodridge Elementary
Untitled. Marker, colored glue, oil pastel
on paper, 12 in. by 8½ in.

C

Monica, *Gone
Swimming.* Woodridge
Elementary, Marker,
tempera, crayon on
paper, 12 in. by
26⅝ in.

gone   swimming
Monica

Art Today

Some artists show movement with photographs.
Which pictures above seem to move?
They are pictures of **motion.**
Where have you seen motion pictures?

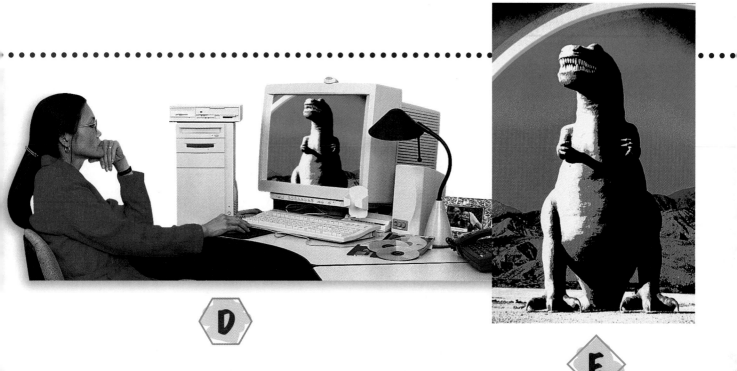

Artists today create in many ways.
Look at **D**.
How does this artist make pictures?
Why do artists try new ways?

Try Your Hand

Think of something that moves.
Maybe it grows or changes.
1. Remember some ways that it moves.
2. Draw how it looks at first.
3. Draw it three more times.
4. Show how it grows or changes.

Art Then and Now

Artists create pictures in storybooks.
Pictures help you better understand the words.
They **illustrate** what the words say.
What words might go with these pictures?

 Frontispiece for *The Baby's Own Aesop* by Walter Crane. Frederick Warne and Co., Ltd.

 Beatrix Potter. *Jemima Puddle-duck and the foxy gentleman*, 1908. Pen, ink, and watercolor.
©1908, 1987, Frederick Warne & Co.

Faith Ringgold. *Bookcover of Tar Beach (Woman on a Beach Series #1)*, 1988. Original art is acrylic paint on canvas bordered with printed and painted quilted and pieced cloth, 74⅝ by 68½ inches. The Solomon R. Guggenheim Museum, New York. Gift of Mr. and Mrs. Gus and Judith Lieber, 1988. Photograph of original art for bookcover by David Heald, ©The Solomon R. Guggenheim Foundation, New York.

Pictures **A** and **B** are old.
Picture **C** is newer than **A** or **B**.
The artists made them to illustrate books.
Which one shows the name of the book?

Planning Like an Artist

I can illustrate my own story.
Which story shall I choose?
I could sketch ideas for pictures.

Laura Smith. *Florida Statehood (150th Statehood Anniversary Stamp)*, issued March 1995. United States Postal Service.

Sheila, Conley Elementary, *Plan for a Postage Stamp*. Torn construction paper on paper, 18 in. by 12 in.

Art Everywhere

You can see art everywhere.
It is on postage stamps.
It is on posters.
Where else can you see art?

 Cerisa Skinner. *A Giant Is Putting Books Into Homes. People Can Read Them, Like Them, Keep Them,* 1996. ©1996 by Reading is Fundamental, Inc. Reprinted with permission.

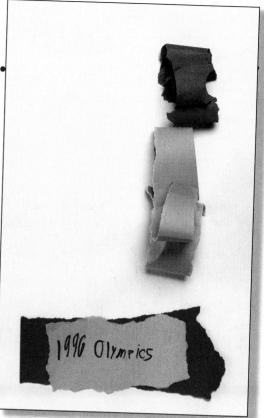

 Marcus, Conley Elementary, *The Olympic.* Torn construction paper on paper, 18 in. by 12 in.

Look at the pictures on these pages.
Each artwork tells you something.
Each picture has meaning.
What is each one about?

Try Your Hand

What means something special to you?
1. Make sketches to plan a poster.
2. Then get a large sheet of paper.
3. Cut shapes and paste them on.
4. You might add a few words.

Buildings Then and Now

Artist unknown. *Cliff Palace, Mesa Verde National Park, Colorado.* ©1996 David Muench.

Look at **A** and **B**.
Which one is older?
Which one is newer?
Artists make plans for buildings.
These artists are called architects.

Point to the buildings in **A**.
They were built into a cliff.
What shapes do you see in **A**?
Do you see forms? Tell where.

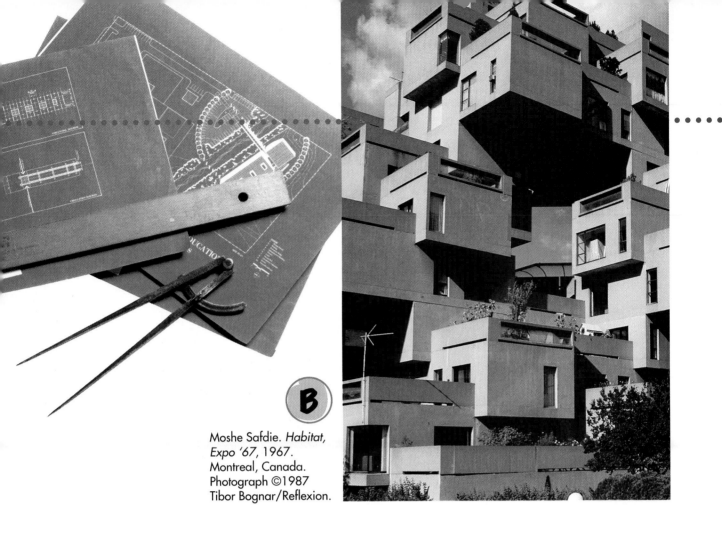

Moshe Safdie. *Habitat, Expo '67*, 1967. Montreal, Canada. Photograph ©1987 Tibor Bognar/Reflexion.

Name the shapes in **B**.
What do the forms look like?
Many people could live in both **A** and **B**.

Thinking Like an Artist

I could become an architect.
I can plan buildings.
My ideas are original.
I can make sketches of my ideas.

Château de By, near Fontainebleau, France. This museum is the former home and studio of Rosa Bonheur.

Art Museums

Most cities have an art **museum.**
Museums have many artworks to view.
Some workers there take care of the art.
Others tell visitors about it.

B

Some museums are old.
Others are newer.
An artist lived in **A.**
Her home became an art museum.
Is the museum old or new?
How can you tell?

C Alex, Katlin, and Eboni, Conley Elementary, *Untitled.* Milk cartons, construction paper, markers, 34½ in. by 11 in. by 15 in.

Elaine, Michael, and Paulina, Conley Elementary, *The Tower Box Museum.* Milk cartons, construction paper, markers, 18 in. by 12 in. by 18 in.

Who makes the plans for new museums?
Architects make **models** to help them plan.
A model of a building is very small.
It can be put on a table.

Try Your Hand

How can you plan a new art museum?
Make a model with your friends.
1. Tape or paste paper onto a milk carton.
2. Draw shapes for windows and doors.
3. Stack your form on your friends' forms.
4. Tape or paste them all together.
How many rooms are in your model?
What could you keep in each room?

Buildings Then and Now   93

PORTFOLIO PROJECT

City at Night

How do cities look at night?

1. Draw buildings with your finger.

2. Then draw them with glue. Let it dry.

3. Color your buildings.

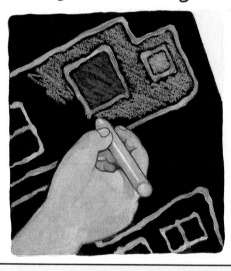

4. Draw shapes of people. Add some cars and lights.

Does your picture show day or night?
What makes it pleasing to the eye?
Would you change anything?

PORTFOLIO GALLERY

A Daryn, Olympia Elementary, *City at Night.* Colored glue, oil pastels on black paper, 18 in. by 12 in.

B Cathryn, Forest Trail Elementary, *Untitled.* Colored glue, oil pastels on black paper, 18 in. by 12 in.

TALK ABOUT ART

Edouard-Louis Dubufe.
Portrait of Rosa Bonheur,
1857. Oil on canvas.
Musèe du Château de
Versailles. © Photo
R.M.N.

Rosa Bonheur, *Rabbits Nibbling
Carrots,* 1840. Oil on canvas, 21¼
by 25½ in. Bordeaux Musée des
Beaux-Arts. Reproduction © Musée
des Beaux-Arts de Bordeaux.

Look at the portrait in **A**.
How is it different from others you've seen?
The artist in **A** loved animals.

The artist in **A** painted **B**.
She painted hundreds of lines for fur.
Tell about the texture of the rabbits.
Point to light colors.
Point to dark ones.
How is the painting balanced?

Ts'ui Po. Detail of *Magpies and Hare*, 960-1279 (Sung Dynasty). Hanging scroll, ink and color on silk. National Palace Museum, Taipei, Taiwan, Republic of China.

The artist of **C** lived far away.
Point to dark and light parts of the hare.
Try to imagine its texture.

Look at the ears in **B** and **C**.
How are they alike?
How are they different?

How can you tell that both artworks are old?
What was each artist trying to say?

Have your feelings about **B** and **C** changed since you first saw them? Explain.

WRITE ABOUT ART

Bonheur grew up in France.

She liked to play outside in the  .

She liked to draw   , and .

These drawings helped her learn to .

She learned to write a C next to each .

She learned to write a B next to each .

Soon she could read and write many A BC.

She stopped writing A BC on her drawings.

But she never stopped painting and drawing.

 Draw a picture of an animal.
Write the name of the animal.
Then write about the animal.
Tell about its color and size.
Tell about where it lives.

What Have You Learned?

Where have you seen these pictures?

Ts'ui Po. Detail of *Magpies and Hare*, 960-1279 (Sung Dynasty). Hanging scroll, ink and color on silk. National Palace Museum, Taipei, Taiwan, Republic of China.

1. Point to straight and curvy lines.
2. What type of artwork is **A**?
3. Point to a soft texture.
4. Can you find a part of an art museum?

5. Which artworks are old?
6. Which one is newer?
7. Name some shapes in **B**.
8. Name the colors in **A**.

9. Which artwork shows a city street?
10. Which art activity did you enjoy? Why?

11. Turn back to the artwork you like best.
12. What else did you learn about art old and new?

Faith Ringgold. *Mrs. Jones and Family*, 1973. Canvas fabric painted and embroidered, 60 by 12 by 16 inches. © Faith Ringgold, Inc. Collection of the artist. Photograph by Karen Bell.

More Ways to Do Art

People have many ways of doing art.
They make artworks for different reasons.

Some artists give beauty to useful things.
They make lovely things to wear.
They build fine rocking chairs.
A few even dress up the alphabet!

Other artists create art about special times.
They show what happened then.

First Look

This artwork shows the artist's family.
Can you find the mother?
Point to the three children.
How does this soft sculpture make you feel?

Art words
mola   jewelry   mask
indoor space   outdoor space
furniture   quilt

Art to Wear

B

C

Artist unknown, Kuna People (Panama). *Mola: The Bell is Placed in the Church*, c.1960. Appliqued embroidered cotton and synthetic fabric, 20¼ by 20⅞ inches. From the Girard Collection in the Museum of International Folk Art, a unit of the Museum of New Mexico, Santa Fe, N.Mex. Photograph by Michel Monteaux.

A

Where have you seen beautiful clothing?
Some artists make lovely things to wear.

An artist made the red **mola** in **A**.
She sewed many shapes together.
They each have special meaning.
She added the blue part to the mola.

Which shapes in **A** can you name?
Where do you see patterns?
What type of balance did the artist use?

D Artist unknown, *Gold bracelet from the "Oxus Treasure,"* 5th century, B.C. Gold, originally inlaid with enamel or stones, height 5 inches. The British Museum, London.

Sydni, Orange Grove Elementary, *The Indian.* Brown paper, construction paper, crayon, 11½ in. by 17½ in.

What kind of **jewelry** is shown in **D**?
It was made a long time ago.
What type of balance did the artist use?
What kinds of jewelry do you like?

Seeing Like an Artist

I can see with my imagination.
I'll draw someone wearing a mola.
I can use many colors.
I'll show shapes and patterns.
Will I add some jewelry?
What do I like about my drawing?

Artist unknown, Eskimo (Yupik). *Mask: Bear Spirit*, late 19th century. Wood, paint, fiber, gut cord. Dallas Museum of Art. Gift of Elizabeth H. Penn.

Artist unknown. *Rabbit Mask*, 19th-20th century. Wood, paint, 15¾ by 5½ by 6¾ inches (40 by 14 by 17.1 cm.). The Metropolitan Museum of Art, Gift of Mr. and Mrs. J. Gordon Douglas III, 1982. (1982.393.2)

Masks

Each of these artworks is a **mask.**
Masks can change the way people look.
Masks can change the way they feel and act.

What animal does **A** look like?
People danced as they wore this mask.
They wore it for special times.
Talk about the balance of **A** and **B**.

1. Fold a paper plate.

2. Cut into the fold.

3. Add many details.

4. Tie it on with yarn.

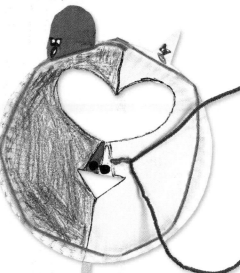

D

Brittany, Conley Elementary, *The Pretty Mask Bee*. Paper plate, marker, 9 in. round

Tell about the texture in **B**.
What animal does **B** look like?
Would you like to wear a mask?
Tell why or why not.

E

Alan, Conley Elementary, *Untitled*. Paper plate, crayon, pipe cleaner, construction paper, 11½ in. by 17 in.

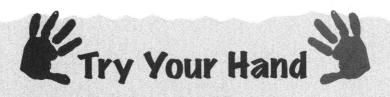

Try Your Hand

Make your own mask.
Will it look like an animal?
How will it change the way you look?
How will it make you act and feel?

Art About Special Times

 Doris Lee (American, 1905-1983). *Thanksgiving*, 1935. Oil on canvas, 28 1/10 by 40 inches (71.4 by 101.6 cm.). The Art Institute of Chicago. Mr. and Mrs. Frank G. Logan Prize Fund. Photograph © The Art Institute of Chicago. All Rights Reserved.1935.313

What day is special to you?
What makes it that way?
Artists make pictures of special times.
They show what happened then.

Picture **A** shows an **indoor space.**
It is about a holiday.
Which holiday do you think it is?
How can you tell?

Carmen Lomas Garza. *Birthday Party,* 1989. Oil on canvas, 36 by 48 inches. Collection of the artist. Photograph: Wolfgang Dietze. From *Family Pictures,* © Carmen Lomas Garza. Reprinted with permission from the publisher, Children's Book Press, San Fransisco, CA.

Picture **B** shows an **outdoor space.**
The artist in **B** showed her own party.
She remembered it from long ago.
What type of party is it?
How do you know?

Planning Like an Artist

I have made pictures of special times.
I could save them for many years.
Someday I could look at them again.
Then I would remember my special times.

 Grandma Moses. *Joy Ride*, 1953. Oil on pressed wood, 18 by 24 inches. Copyright © 1992, Grandma Moses Properties Co., New York

Seasons and Storms

Which seasons can you name?
Name the season that **A** shows.
How can you tell?
Point to movement in **A**.

 Amir, Conley Elementary, *A Snowy Day.* Construction paper, 17½ in. by 11½ in.

What is **C** about?
What do you think the tiger wants?
Is the space indoors or outdoors?
How do you know a storm has come?
Talk about the movement in **C**.

Try Your Hand

What is your favorite season?
1. Paint a picture of that season.
2. Use some torn-paper shapes, too.
3. Will you show movement?

Art About Special Times **109**

Art to See and Use

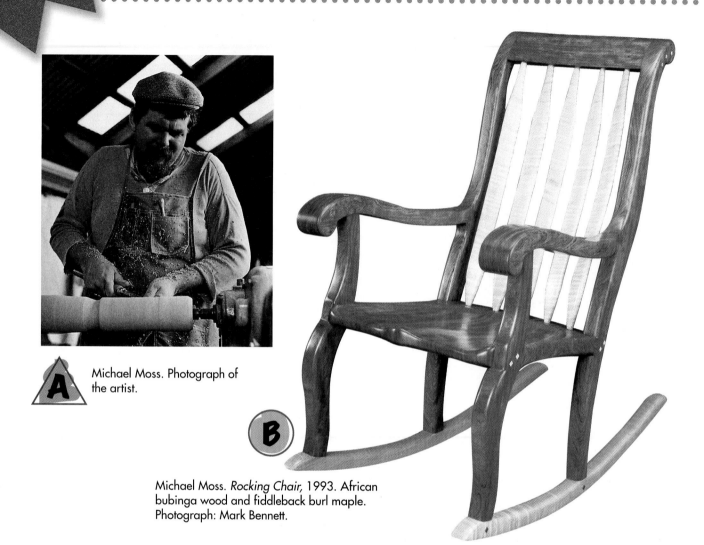

A Michael Moss. Photograph of the artist.

B Michael Moss. *Rocking Chair,* 1993. African bubinga wood and fiddleback burl maple. Photograph: Mark Bennett.

Have you ever sat in a rocking chair?
A good rocking chair feels just right.
The texture is smooth.
The form fits your body.
The movement can rock you to sleep.

The artist in **A** made **B**.
He builds other types of **furniture**, too.

San Antonio Needlework Guild. *Bicentennial Quilt*, 1976. Appliqued cotton, 107 by 73 inches. The Witte Museum.

Many artists worked together to make **C**.
Each one sewed a block.
Then they sewed all the blocks together.
The whole artwork is called a **quilt.**
Where have you seen a quilt?

Thinking Like an Artist

Do I like to work alone?
Do I like to work with friends?
Which art projects can I do alone?
Which ones can I do with friends?

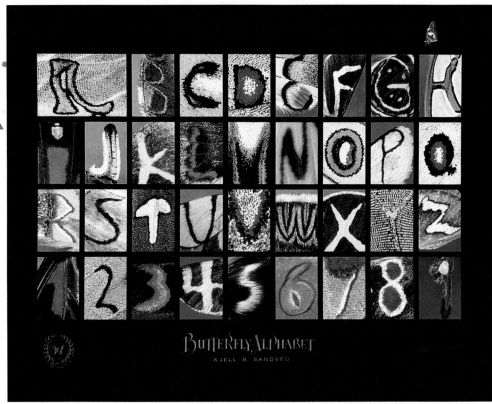

Artists and the Alphabet

Some artists create with letters.
The artist of **A** dressed up the whole alphabet.
Where did he find these letters?
What is the artist trying to say?

B

Diego, Campbell Elementary,
The Pink-eared Tiger. Tempera on paper, 12 in. by 18 in.

D Jennifer, Campbell Elementary, *Animal in a World*. Tempera on paper, 18 in. by 12 in.

E Ebony, Campbell Elementary, *C is for Cat*. Tempera on paper, 12 in. by 18 in.

C Trina Schart Hyman. *Illustration showing the letter "A" in A Little Alphabet*. *Books of Wonder*, William Morrow & Company, New York. © 1980, 1993 by Trina Schart Hyman.

Now look at **C**.
How is **C** different from **A**?
How are all of the artworks alike?
What is special about each artwork?

Try Your Hand

How will you show the alphabet?
1. Choose a letter.
2. Plan how to dress it up.
3. Draw or paint it in an original way.
   Will you work with your friends?
   You could make a book together.
   Your teacher can show you how.

Making a Story Quilt Together
What does your family like to do?

1. Draw a special time with your family.

2. Plan a quilt with three friends. Think of a name for it.

3. Paste down your picture.

4. Make patterns with triangles. Add the name to the top.

Did you like working alone?
Did you like working with your friends?
How do all four drawings look together?

PORTFOLIO GALLERY

Jeffrey, Jessie, Grey, and Brian, Dripping Springs Primary School, *Our Families.* Marker on index cards, construction paper, 18 in. by 12 in.

Sarah, Jessica, Tina, and David, Woodridge Elementary, *Our Families.* Marker, oil pastels on index cards, construction paper, 18 in. by 12 in.

TALK ABOUT ART

Who is the artist in **A**?
Her own painting is behind her.
It is a part of a quilt she made.
The quilt tells a story about her life.

A C' Love. *Portrait of Faith Ringgold with detail of "The Purple Quilt,"* Photograph, © C' Love, 1986.

B Faith Ringgold. *Mrs. Jones and Family,* 1973. Canvas fabric painted and embroidered, 60 by 12 by 16 inches. ©Faith Ringgold, Inc. Collection of the artist. Photograph by Karen Bell.

The artist in **A** also creates soft sculptures.
The sculptures in **B** show her family.
Find the three children and their mother.

She made the faces look like masks.
How did she create the clothes?
Point to patterns on the clothes.

Elizabeth Catlett. *Mother and Child,* 1971. Cedar, height 26 inches. ©1998 Elizabeth Catlett, licensed by VAGA, New York.

The sculpture in **C** shows a mother and child. How do they feel about each other? How do the lines help you see this?

How is **C** like **B**? How are **C** and **B** different?

What were both artists trying to say? Have your feelings about **B** and **C** changed since you first saw them? Explain.

WRITE ABOUT ART

As a child **Faith Ringgold** played with  .

She used  , a  , and .

She made tiny  , , and  .

Now  uses in her artworks.

She sews cloth .

She makes cloth ▢ ▢ for her paintings.

She even 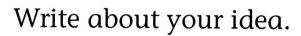 across some of her paintings.

These artworks tell stories about her life.

Look at **B** on page 116.
It shows the artist's family.
Look at the colorful cloth.
What could you make with cloth?

Write about your idea.

What Have You Learned?

Where have you seen these pictures?

1. Point to a close-up view of a quilt.
2. What is important in **C**?
3. How does the artist show this?
4. Is this an indoor or an outdoor space?

5. Point to the close-up view of a mola.
6. Tell about the patterns you see in it.
7. Why is the bird larger than the house?

8. What is happening in **B**?
9. What shapes are on the floor?
10. How does the artist show movement?

11. Turn back to the artwork you like best. Tell why.
12. What else have you learned about more ways to do art?

Artist unknown, Kuna People (Panama). *Mola: The Bell is Placed in the Church,* c.1960. Appliqued embroidered cotton and synthetic fabric, 20¼ by 20⅞ inches. From the Girard Collection in the Museum of International Folk Art, a unit of the Museum of New Mexico, Santa Fe, N.Mex. Photograph by Michel Monteaux.

Doris Lee (American, 1905-1963). *Thanksgiving,* 1935. Oil on canvas, 28¹⁄₁₀ by 40 inches (71.4 by 101.6 cm.). The Art Institute of Chicago. Mr. and Mrs. Frank G. Logan Prize Fund. Photograph © The Art Institute of Chicago. All Rights Reserved.1935.313

San Antonio Needlework Guild. *Bicentennial Quilt,* 1976. Appliqued cotton, 107 by 73 inches. The Witte Museum.

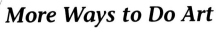

More Ways to Do Art **119**

Think Safety

Look at the pictures on these pages.
They show children using art materials safely.

Then read the safety rules.
Follow these rules when you make artworks.

1. **Keep art materials away from your mouth.**

2. **Keep art materials away from your eyes.**

3. **Do not breathe chalk dust or art sprays.**

4. **Look for the word nontoxic on labels. This means the materials are safe to use.**

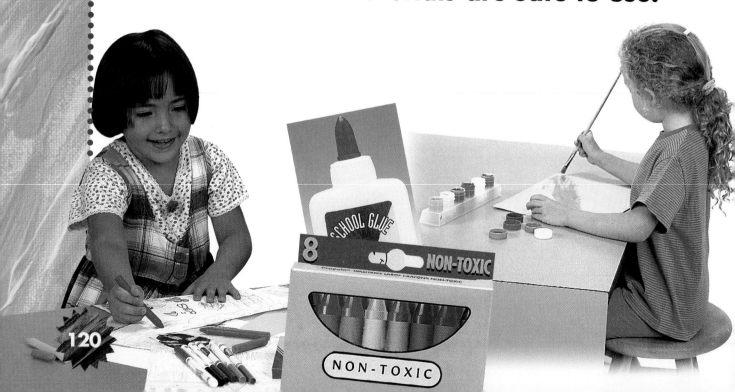

5. **Always use safety scissors. Take care with all sharp objects.**

6. **Use only new meat trays and egg cartons.**

7. **Wash your hands when you finish an artwork.**

8. **If you have a problem, get help from your teacher.**

 Can you think of more ways to be safe?

Picture Glossary

architect
Page 73

artwork
Page 8

balance
Page 66

camera
Page 82

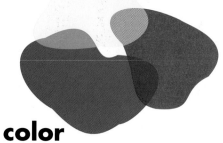

color
Page 10

cool colors
Page 30

detail
Page 29

face
Page 69

form
Page 42

furniture
Page 110

illustrate
Page 86

indoor space
Page 106

jewelry
Page 103

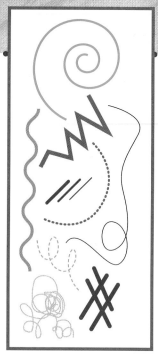

line
Page 2

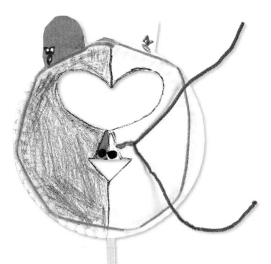

mask
Page 104

model
Page 93

mola
Page 102

motion
Page 84

movement
Page 46

museum
Page 92

original
Page 51

outdoor space
Page 107

pattern
Page 26

photograph
Page 82

portrait
Page 68

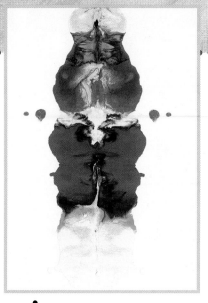

print
Page 67

puppet
Page 50

quilt
Page 111

sculptor
Page 44

sculpture
Page 44

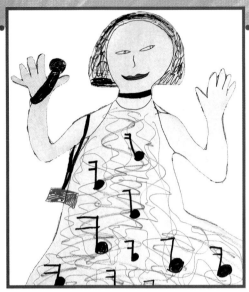

self-portrait
Page 68

shape
Page 6

symmetrical balance
Page 66

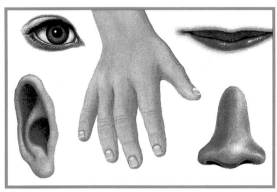

senses
Page 65

space
Page 42

texture
Page 22

warm colors
Page 30

Portfolios **127**

Index

ACKNOWLEDGMENTS

CONTRIBUTORS

The author and publisher wish to thank the following teachers for their contributions to the development of ideas and procedures for art activities and projects in this series:

Martha Camacho, Wanza Coates, Joan Elder, Kelly Fox, Lisa Fuentes, Maureen Clare Gillis, Karen Johnson, Joan Klasson, Leisa M. Koch, Lara Landers, Tamera S. Moore, Sharon R. Nagy, Teri Evans-Palmer, Julie Pohlmann, Jean Powell, Cynde Riddle, Nancy J. Sass, Lori Schimmel, Melissa St. John, Sue Telle, Susan Urband, Fatima Usrey, Pamela Valentine, Caryl E. Williams

We appreciate the efforts of the following teachers who graciously submitted student art for use in this series:

Wanza Coates, Linda Caitlin, Joan Elder, Kelly Fox, Karen Johnson, Joan Klasson, Dottie Myers, Julie Pohlmann, Jean Powell, Dana Reyna, Nancy J. Sass, Lori Schimmel, Ingrid Sherwood, Melissa St. John, Tammy Suarez, Marie Swope, Sue Telle, Susan Urband, Fatima Usrey, Marilyn Wylie, Jamie Wood

We wish to thank the following teachers for their expertise, wisdom, and wholehearted good will during the field testing of this series:

Sammie Gray, Mary Alice Lopez, Robin Maca, Deborah McLouth, Lois Pendley, Dana Reyna, Ingrid Sherwood, Sue Telle, Marilyn Wylie

We gratefully acknowledge the following schools for allowing us to work with their teachers and students during the development of this series:

Conley Elementary, Aldine Independent School District; Roosevelt Elementary, San Antonio Independent School District; Amelia Earhart Learning Center, Dallas Independent School District; Cedar Creek Elementary, Eanes Independent School District; Smith Elementary, Alief Independent School District; Heflin Elementary, Alief Independent School District; Hill Elementary, Austin Independent School District; Odom Elementary, Austin Independent School District; Brooke Elementary, Austin Independent School District; Campbell Elementary, Austin Independent School District; Zavala Elementary, Austin Independent School District; Langford Elementary, Austin Independent School District; Brentwood Elementary, Austin Independent School District; Burnet Elementary, San Antonio Independent School District; Edgewater Elementary, Anne Arundel County Public Schools; Landis Elementary, Alief Independent

School District; Boone Elementary, Alief Independent School District; College of Fine Art, Maryland Institute, Baltimore, Maryland; Orange Grove Elementary, Aldine Independent School District; Klentzman Intermediate School, Alief Independent School District; Forest Trail Elementary, Eanes Independent School District; Teague Middle School, Aldine Independent School District; Martin Elementary, Alief Independent School District; Petrosky Elementary, Alief Independent School District; North Hi Mount Elementary, Fort Worth Independent School District; Cambridge Elementary, Alamo Heights Independent School District; Porter Elementary, Birdville Independent School District; Woodridge Elementary, Alamo Heights Independent School District; Anderson Academy, Aldine Independent School District; Creative Fine Arts Magnet School, San Francisco Unified School District; Wonderland School, San Marcos, Texas; Olsen Park Elementary, Amarillo Independent School District; Liestman Elementary, Alief Independent School District; Hogg Elementary, Dallas Independent School District; Bivins Elementary, Amarillo Independent School District; Tuckahoe Elementary, Arlington Public Schools, Fine Arts Department of North East Independent School District; Fox Hill Elementary, Indianapolis Public Schools.

A special acknowledgment to the founders of the SHARE program in San Antonio, Texas, Pamela Valentine and Sue Telle, who graciously allowed us to share with the world their prized and inspirational student artwork. The SHARE (Students Help Art Reach Everyone) program is a foundation dedicated to students and their art, and develops opportunities for students to interact with and enlighten their community.

A final acknowledgment to Barrett and Kendall, the inspiration behind State of the Art.

PHOTO CREDITS

Key: (t) top, (c) center, (b) bottom, (l) left, (r) right.

Table of contents: Page v, vi, Barrett Kendall photos by Andrew Yates; vii(l), SuperStock; vii(r), W. K. Fletcher/PhotoResearchers, Inc.; viii, David Young-Wolff/PhotoEdit; ix, Dennis MacDonald/PhotoEdit.

UNIT 1. Page xii, 16(cr), 19(tr), © 1997 Artists Rights Society (ARS), New York/ADAGP, Paris; 1(l), Nio-Hays; 1(r), Barrett Kendall photo by Andrew Yates; 2(tr), Barrett Kendall photo by Peter van Steen; 2(l), David Young-Wolff/PhotoEdit; 2(cr), Michael Newman/PhotoEdit; 4, 19(tl) © 1998 Estate of Pablo Picasso/Artists Rights Society (ARS), New York; 6(tl, tr), Barrett Kendall photos by Peter van Steen; 6(bl), Larry Gatz/The Image Bank; 6(cr), SuperStock; 8, 19(tc), © Earlie Hudnall; 10, Peter Correz/Tony Stone Images. 13, photograph © 1996 Sotheby's Inc., New York.

UNIT 2. Page 21(tr, c), Nio-Hays; 21(cr), Barrett Kendall photo by Andrew Yates; 22(tl), Nio-Hays; 22(tr), David Young-Wolff/PhotoEdit; 22(bl), Barrett Kendall photo by Andrew Yates; 22(bc), © SuperStock; 22(br), David Young-Wolff/PhotoEdit; 25(tl), © 1993 Sotheby's. Inc.; 26(tl), Jonathan Nourio/PhotoEdit; 26(c), SuperStock; 28(t), Nio-Hays; 30(tl), Steve Skjold/Lightwave; 30(tr), Nio-Hays; 30(tr/inset), Richard Hutchings/PhotoEdit; 30(bl), 31(tr), Nio-Hays; 31(cr), SuperStock; 33, © 1998 Estate of Pablo Picasso/Artists Rights Society (ARS), New York.

UNIT 3. Page 46(tl), 46(r), 46(bl), SuperStock; 47(tl), Jose Carillo/PhotoEdit; 47(bl), Barrett Kendall photo by Andrew Yates; 49, Nio-Hays; 53(tl), Mary Kate Denny/PhotoEdit; 57 © 1997 Estate of Pablo Picasso/Artists Rights Society (ARS), New York.

UNIT 4. Page 66(cl), SuperStock; 68(tl), Nio-Hays; 70(tl), David W. Hamilton/The Image Bank; 70(bl), Benn Mitchell/The Image Bank; 72(tr), 79(tr) © 1998 Artists Rights Society (ARS), New York/VG Bild Kunst, Bonn; 73, Michael Newman/PhotoEdit.

UNIT 5. Page 82(l), Corbis/Bettmann Archives; 82(r), Austin History Center, Austin Public Library; 83(t), Barrett Kendall photo by Peter van Steen; 83(b), Barrett Kendall photo by Andrew Yates; 84, 85(l), Barrett Kendall photo by Peter van Steen; 85(r), Garry Gay/The Image Bank; 87, photograph by David Heald, © The Solomon R. Guggenhiem Foundation, New York; 86, 88(b), Barrett Kendall photo by Andrew Yates; 92(t), Princeton University Libraries, Marquant Library; 92(b), Katheryn Davidson, Austin Museum of Art; 99(l), Barrett Kendall photo by Peter van Steen; 99(c), Princeton University Libraries, Marquant Library.

UNIT 6. Page 102(tr), David R. Frazier; 102(cr), Texas Department of Commerce/Tourism; 110(tr), photograph by Frederica Georgia, © Southern Living, Inc. Reprinted with permission; 111, Nio-Hays; 113, (tl) by permission of Morrow Junior Books, a division of William Morrow and Company.

Page 120-121, Barrett Kendall photograph by Andrew Yates ; 124(br), Barrett Kendall photograph by Peter van Steen; 125(tl), Superstock, (tr), Kathryn Davidson, Austin Museum of Art, (br), Barrett Kendall photograph by Peter van Steen; 127(br), Nio-Hays

© Photodisc, Inc. pages, i-iv background; x, xi, 4(tl), 8(tl), 12(tl), 14(bl), 24(tl), 32(tl), 41(t,m), 44(tl), 48(tl), 52(tl), 61(tr), 64(tl), 66(r), 70, 72(tl), 81(l,tr), 84(tl), 86(bl), 91(tl), 92(tl), 104(tl), 108(tl), 112(tl), 122(ml,mr), 123(bl), 124(tl), 107(mr), 127(mr).

I L L U S T R A T I O N   C R E D I T S

Holly Cooper: 27, 34, 67, 74, 78, 105, 114, 118

Jim Effler: 1, 42

Doug Henry: 122, 123, 124, 126, 127

Mike Krone: 11, 14, 18, 23, 38, 51, 54, 58, 94, 98, 123

Kevin Peake: 66, 68, 72

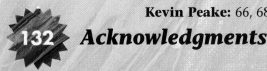